EVEREST CLIMB
To the Top of the World

Robyn P. Watts

Teacher Notes:

Sir Edmund Hillary and Sherpa Tenzing Norgay became the first mountaineers to successfully summit the highest mountain in the world, Mount Everest. Learn about the challenges they faced and the importance of preparation, training, and determination in their quest to succeed. Discover how equipment has changed and how tourism is affecting this very special part of the world.

Discussion points for consideration:

1. How important was Sir Edmund Hillary and Tenzing Norgay's fierce determination to succeed?

2. Climbing Mt Everest takes huge preparation, training, goal-setting, hard work, determination, and resilience. Discuss these further and how they can help you in everyday life.

3. What are the pros and cons of allowing mountaineering and tourism on and around Mt Everest? Consider the country's economy, the environment and the potential danger.

Sight words, difficult to decode words, and infrequent words to be introduced and practiced before reading this book:

Everest, dangerous, Tibetan, Nepalese, Sagarmatha, Sherpas, Chomolungma, impossible, avalanche, oxygen, New Zealander, Sir Edmund Hillary, Tenzing Norgay, Kathmandu, expedition, descend, acclimatizing, altitude, equipment, crevasses, elevation, fervent, cornice, considerable, determination, exhausted, attitude, aluminium, handknitted, crampons, attachments, insulation, balaclava, frostbite, waterproof, carabiners, exposure, Japanese, mountaineer.

Contents

1. About Mount Everest

Mt Everest is the highest mountain in the world. It sits on the border between Nepal and Tibet. How high is Mt Everest? Mt Everest is 8,848 metres high. This is 29,028 feet!

Many people would like to climb Mt Everest. At one stage there were so many people climbing, they had to limit the numbers. People were lining up to do the climb for hours. This became very dangerous.

Now you have to book ahead to stop people waiting to reach the top of the mountain. Mt Everest is still a very deadly mountain. It is not easy to climb, and things go wrong all the time.

The Tibetans and the Nepalese have another name for Mt Everest.

In Nepal, Mt Everest is known as the "Sky's Head."

The local Sherpas and the Tibetans who live around Mt Everest call the mountain the "Goddess of the Wind."

The names of the mountain suggest that it is high in the sky. The wind can affect the success of a climb. If it is too windy the climbers stop their climb of Mt Everest.

Scan this QR code to see a YouTube video about the history of the climb of Mt Everest.

Mt Everest was not climbed until 1953. It was thought to be an impossible climb.

Before 1953, people tried to find a way to the top. They had to find a route that would not end in a big cliff or rock face. They spent many years mapping to try and find the best way to the top.

Why was Mt Everest a dangerous climb? It is a very dangerous climb because of the deep snow which falls. This snow builds up and then falls down the mountain.

The second problem is the lack of oxygen. At the top of Mt Everest, the oxygen is only one third the normal amount. This makes it hard to breathe on high mountains.

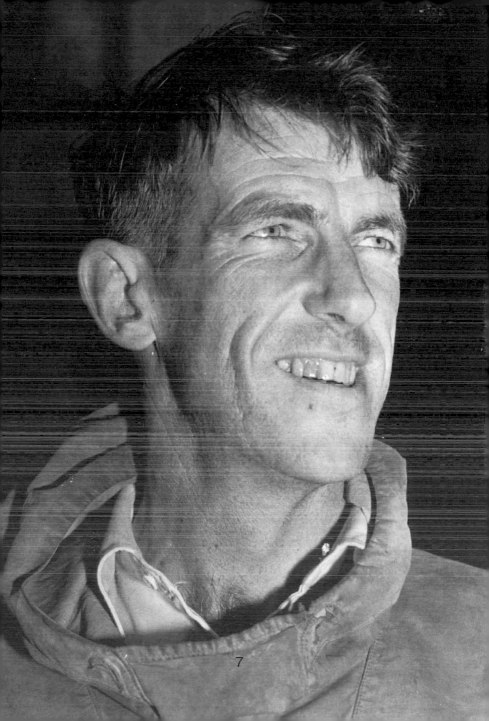

2. Climbing Mount Everest

Who was the first person to climb Mt Everest? Sir Edmund Hillary, a New Zealander, and Tenzing Norgay, a Nepalese Sherpa, first climbed to the top.

Sir Edmund Hillary was 33 years old when he made the first step on to the summit, followed by Sherpa Tenzing Norgay.

The weather only allows a small amount of time and the route to the top had to be found. Everything worked this time and they made it to the top.

9

3. At the Summit

They stayed at the summit for 15 minutes. Hillary took a photograph of Tenzing to show the moment. There were no selfies with cameras in 1953.

Hillary left a cross on top, and Norgay left an offering of chocolates.

They reached the summit at eleven thirty in the morning. They needed to make sure they could get down again before darkness. Their oxygen supply was low so they couldn't stay long.

What would you think about if you were standing on the highest peak in the world for fifteen minutes?

The expedition with four hundred people left Kathmandu in 1953 and took seven weeks to complete. There were three hundred porters, twenty Sherpa guides and about four and a half tons of baggage. The last part of the journey close to the summit took five hours to complete. During the expedition, the crew often faced snow and wind which stopped their climb. The four climbers were broken up into teams. Hillary and Tenzing were in one team. The trip up the mountain was very difficult and when they neared the summit, only four men were able to continue. Bourdillon and Evans got to only 300 feet from the top. They then had to turn back because Evans' oxygen system stopped working.

Hillary was paired with Sherpa Tenzing Norgay and they made the final attempt to reach the summit.

You can hear the audio of Sir Edmund Hillary telling the story himself.

By walking slowly and steadily towards Mt Everest from Kathmandu, the trekkers had time to strengthen their muscles. By walking slowly, they could get used to being at higher altitudes. There are many Sherpa villages you pass through while walking on the trek. Sherpas have spent all their life in the mountains. The Sherpas have been living and walking at high altitudes for a long time.

4. Sherpas

Many Sherpas are needed as guides to climb Mt Everest. The Sherpas are hired to carry food and equipment. The Sherpas do the cooking, prepare the climbers' rope pathways, and use ladders for bridges across the ice crevasses. Tenzing Norgay was a Sherpa.

On the Tibetan side of Mt Everest, the Chinese have built a highway all the way to the northern Everest Base Camp. This Base Camp is at an altitude of 17,600 feet. This does not mean it is easier to climb Mt Everest as you still need to adjust to the height and low oxygen.

What approach to Mt Everest would you choose? Here is what Sir Edmund Hillary wrote in an article describing the last part of the climb near the summit.

"I walked backwards up the crack, with a fervent prayer that the cornice would remain attached to the rock. Despite the considerable effort involved, my progress although slow was steady, and as Tenzing paid out the rope I inched my way upwards until I could finally reach over the top of the rock and drag myself out of the crack on to a wide ledge."

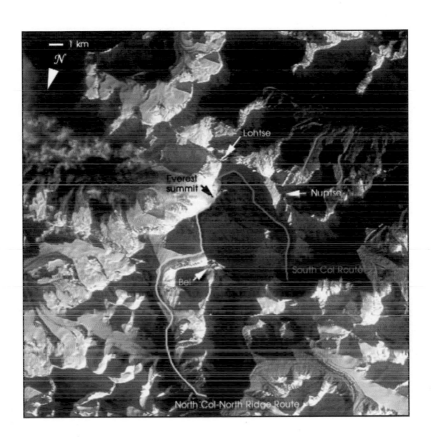

Lohtse

Everest summit

Nuptse

South Col Route

Bel

North Col-North Ridge Route

"For a few moments I lay regaining my breath and for the first time really felt the fierce determination that nothing now could stop us from reaching the top. I took a firm stand on the ledge and signalled to Tenzing to come on up. As I heaved hard on the rope Tenzing wriggled his way up the crack and finally collapsed exhausted at the top like a giant fish when it has just been hauled from the sea after a terrific struggle."

5. Never Giving Up!

Did you notice that Sir Edmund Hillary had a great sense of determination? Determination is that "go for it" attitude. It is knowing that you have a chance to win, either as a team, group, or individually, if you just give it your all. Since the first ascent of Mt Everest, many others have made it to the summit. The youngest was just 13 and the oldest was over 80.

Whatever we do, we can choose to fight to succeed. There are very few people that are just lucky enough to strike success. Most people put in a great effort and hope they can also be lucky to win. And to keep winning means more and more work.

6. Equipment

What type of gear do trekkers need today when climbing Mt Everest?

When Edmund Hillary and Tenzing Norgay climbed Mt. Everest, they had to build snow steps close to the summit. They had to use an ice axe to dig through the snow at the summit and build steps.

Ice Axe An ice axe is a useful tool to build ice steps and is used for ice climbing. In 1953, the ice axe was made of steel and had a wooden handle. Now it is made of lightweight aluminum and is much lighter to carry. Most climbers carry an ice axe.

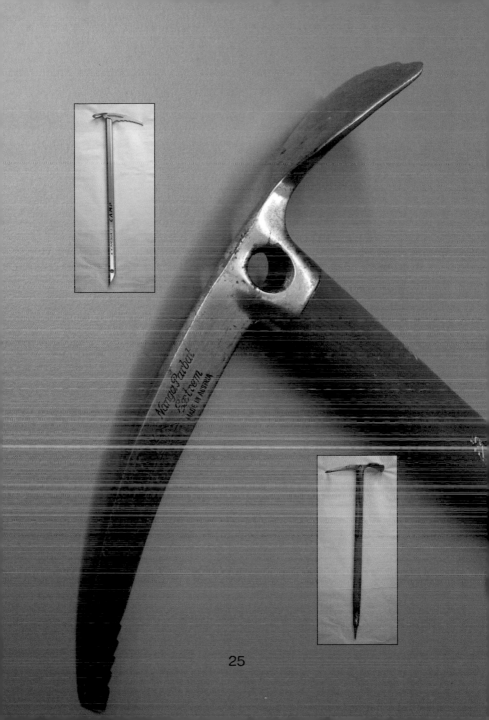

25

Helmets In 1953 they did not use helmets. Today, mountain climbers use lightweight helmets. Hillary wore a handknitted sun helmet made by his sister, and Norgay wore a hat with a brim. The hat was similar to the wide brim hats you wear to school.

Crampons or Ice Spikes Crampons are special spike attachments you add to your boots. They are used for secure travel for walking on snow and ice. They have spikes that give better grip when walking in icy conditions. You attach the crampons to your walking boots. This allows the climber to better grip the snow and ice.

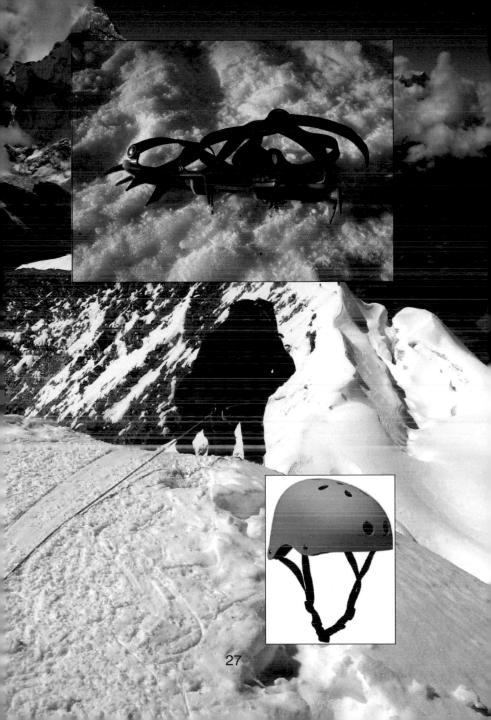

Sunglasses How did Edmund Hillary and Sherpa Tenzing Norgay protect their eyes from the Sun? They kept their goggles on their face by tying them to their heads with a head strap. These days they have lightweight snow googles that stop UV rays entering the eyes.

Sleeping gear Where do mountain climbers sleep? They sleep in sleeping bags in tents. The tents have to be strong enough to protect them from strong winds.

Sleeping bags are very light. They have a nylon outer shell. Goose down filling is used to stop the cold getting inside the sleeping bag.

Balaclava What is a balaclava? It is a close-fitting garment which covers the whole head, neck, and parts of the face. It has holes for the nose and the mouth. It covers your ears, and in icy conditions, it is usually made of wool. It protects your head, neck, and face and keeps you warm.

Oxygen Tanks These are needed to climb Mt Everest. It is important to know which goggles, balaclavas, and hats work well with your oxygen mask. Very few people have climbed Mt Everest without oxygen. When a climber is having problems breathing, it is better if the climber goes down in altitude. When a climber gets sick from the high altitude, it is important that the lives of other climbers and Sherpas are not put at risk.

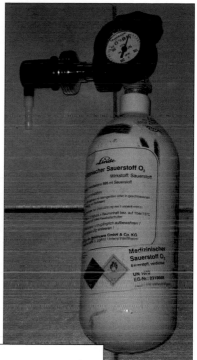

Comms and Phones These days, you can communicate with mobile phones even when climbing Mt Everest. However, in 1953 Edmund Hillary and Tenzing Norgay carried heavy walkie talkies and dry cell batteries.

Boots Most people carry two pairs of boots on the expedition. One pair for climbing and one pair at night to keep their feet warm. The boots are insulated to keep the feet warm and stop frostbite. The boots are also waterproof and lightweight. Why is it important to use waterproof boots? The boots are waterproof so that no ice or snow can touch the skin. The boots are insulated so that the feet are kept warm.

Boots and frostbite? Frostbite occurs when the skin is exposed to extreme cold. The skin freezes and the underlying tissues freeze. The skin becomes cold and red, then the tissues become numb, hard, and pale. The most common areas that need to be protected from frostbite are fingers, ears, nose, cheeks, toes, and the chin.

Gloves Hand gloves are waterproof and insulated for warmth to prevent frostbite. These are strapped on to stop them falling off. Some climbers also wear a thinner pair underneath the outer glove. This helps trap warmth and also helps drive out any sweat.

Ropes and Climbing Straps During an expedition, climbers use ropes, climbing straps and carabiners to help them climb the mountain. What is a carabiner? It is a piece of metal that is used for clipping rope to the gear you are carrying. Carabiners are used to help climbers attach ropes to different pieces of equipment. They are a very handy tool and help keep climbers safe.

Anchors Most climbers use anchors. Anchor points are used to securely attach to a rock or stable point. The anchor points can be hammered into the rock or any other stable feature on the cliff. Ropes are then attached to the anchor point.

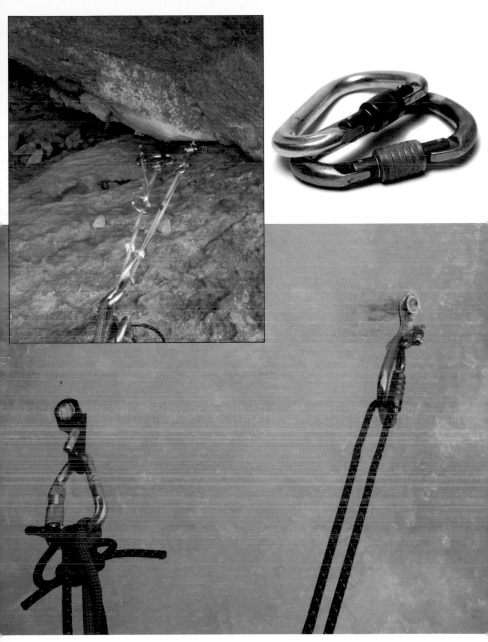

7. Altitude Sickness

Some people suffer altitude sickness more than others. It is a dreadful feeling of a headache and feeling like you are going to vomit. It is there the whole time for some people. Trying to climb is nearly impossible as you cannot breathe properly. Your head feels like it is going to explode. You just want to lie down and go to sleep. This is when people die.

The area above 26,000 feet from Camp 4 to the summit is called the "death zone". The "death zone" is where the air is very thin, and the weather can be very brutal at this altitude. The oxygen levels at the top are only a third of what they are at sea level. Oxygen helps a lot but not always.

When climbing in this area of the mountain, you take ten steps forward then stop and breathe oxygen. When breathing oxygen, a mask is put over the nose and mouth like a snorkel. Each trekker carries their own oxygen tanks.

Most deaths in this zone are due to health problems related to conditions on the mountain, collapse, frost bite, avalanches, falls and exposure to high altitude and winds. Not all bodies have been located, so the reason of death is not always known. There are still over 200 bodies left on Mt Everest. On 25 April, 2015, 22 climbers lost their lives at Base Camp when an earthquake triggered an avalanche that wiped out several expeditions.

8. Women Climbers

One of the first people to use goose down to make her own sleeping bag was a Japanese woman. This woman purchased goose feather from China and made her own sleeping bag. Her name was Junko Tabei, and she was a Japanese mountaineer. She was the first woman to climb Mt Everest in 1975. She chose to walk the same route as Sir Edmund Hillary and Tenzing Norgay. The women's group was camping at 6,300 meters when an avalanche struck their camp. The women and their guides were buried under the snow.

Junko Tabei was caught in the avalanche. She reported later that she was lucky to be alive and only survived due to her Sherpa, Ang Tsering.

Sherpa Ang Tsering dug her out of the snow. She later reported she was knocked out for about six minutes until her Sherpa dug her out. Twelve days after the avalanche, with her Sherpa guide Ang Tsering, Junko Tabei became the first woman to reach the summit of Mt Everest.

Every year there are more and more women climbing Mt Everest.

Word Bank

avalanche	dangerous
Everest	oxygen
Sherpa	breathe
summit	mountains
Hillary	Tenzing Norgay
altitude	weather
carabiners	photograph
mountaineer	chocolates
cornice	attitude
aluminum	expedition
insulation	Kathmandu
Tibetans	delayed
impossible	Bourdillon
route	Nepalese